CW01664206

POE
SAFARI

Leicestershire And Northamptonshire

Edited By Vicki Skelton

First published in Great Britain in 2017 by:

YoungWriters Est. 1991

Coltsfoot Drive
Peterborough
PE2 9BF
Telephone: 01733 890066
Website: www.youngwriters.co.uk

All Rights Reserved
Book Design by Spencer Hart
© Copyright Contributors 2016
SB ISBN 978-1-78624-821-3
Printed and bound in the UK by BookPrintingUK
Website: www.bookprintinguk.com
YB0299O

Clumsy Monkey

Clumsy monkey in the tree being funny,
clumsy and being a monkey like me.
The monkey jumps out of the tree, goes in
the warm pond, relaxed as can be,
The cheeky monkey jumps out of the pond,
goes to a tree and hugs the tree as sweet
as a bee.
I turn around to look at the tigers, I turn
back, where is clumsy monkey?
I peek through a bush and there he is, he is
snug as a bug asleep, giving himself a
big hug,
So I pick him up and one, two, three, he is
jumping around again just like a flea.

Halle Olivia Hands (7)
Barrow Hall Orchard CE Primary School, Loughborough

Cheeky Monkey

The cheeky monkey stole bananas from
other monkeys
They got very cross
The monkey giggled and said, 'You will
never get them back
because I will eat them all.'
The other monkeys had to find more
bananas to eat
When the monkeys had finished the
bananas he was very fat
When he had eaten all of the bananas he
couldn't go out
because he was too fat
If he goes out he will eat more bananas.

Matilda Radburn (5)
Barrow Hall Orchard CE Primary School, Loughborough

The Funky Monkey

Monkeys are funky, they swing everywhere
Monkeys are funky, chunky and funny
This monkey likes to swing
I can sometimes hear him sing
Chunky monkey in the tree
Climbing higher than a flea
Mischievous monkey in the jungle
Swinging up to the sky
Crazy and lazy, eating nuts all day
Cheeky monkey likes to play
Swings around everywhere.

Caitlin Clarke (6)
Barrow Hall Orchard CE Primary School, Loughborough

Crazy Monkey

Chunky monkey is funky and he lives in a
home full of bananas and nuts
He is lazy and crazy
He swings on the trees in the sky
He likes playing in the trees
He is a mischievous guy
He always waves to me when I go to school
He is cute and cuddly
I like stroking his back because it is furry,
hairy and soft.

Scarlet Brookes (6)
Barrow Hall Orchard CE Primary School, Loughborough

Elephant

E lephants' trunk swing side to side
L ikes to splash water everywhere
E normous grey ears
P icks berries from up high
H e stomps the ground on a big walk
A round the big jungle
N uts are its favourite treat
T eaching its baby how to shake a tree.

Daria Budzik (6)
Barrow Hall Orchard CE Primary School, Loughborough

Elephant

E lephants have enormous trunks
L ong tusks
E normous eyes
P ouring water from the river
H e stomps his feet in the muddy mud
A n elephant has great big feet
N uts are its favourite treat
T he elephant walks proudly through the
jungle.

Eva Sleath (7)
Barrow Hall Orchard CE Primary School, Loughborough

The Funky Monkey

Monkeys are funky, chunky and funny
They eat bananas just like we do
Yellow like lemons that are sour
Swinging from trees with monkey flies
Swinging with monkeys is lots of fun
We love them, we love every one
This monkey is funny and swings in the sky
He is a very mischievous guy.

Elizabeth Earl (6)
Barrow Hall Orchard CE Primary School, Loughborough

The Cheekiest Monkey In The World

The funky monkey was in a tree
Higher than I could see
He fell off and bumped his head
So he went to his bed
The funky monkey was on a beach
Eating coconuts and said,
'I might have a paddle.'
So the funky monkey went in the water
But he didn't know how to swim.

Charlie Wareham (7)
Barrow Hall Orchard CE Primary School, Loughborough

Elly The Elephant

E normous grey animals
L ong, wavy trunk
E ars that flap around to keep them cool
P ouring water from the river
H e stomps around looking for food
A mazed how big he is
N ight-time the elephants sleep
T ogether in a heap.

Isaac Hammond (6)
Barrow Hall Orchard CE Primary School, Loughborough

The Cheesy Monkey

The funky monkey was climbing the tree
Peeling banana skins as funny as me
Clumsy, clumsy, down we go all the way
back home
The mischievous monkey swinging
Right through the day and through
the night
The massive monkey being lazy
Got no nuts, so went crazy.

Emily Batts (7)
Barrow Hall Orchard CE Primary School, Loughborough

The Poems

Woodford CE Primary School, Kettering

Contents

Foreword

Dear Reader,

Welcome to this book packed full of feathery, furry and scaly friends!

Young Writers' Poetry Safari competition was specifically designed for 5-7 year-olds as a fun introduction to poetry and as a way to think about the world of animals. They could write about pets, exotic animals, dinosaurs and you may even find a few crazy creatures that have never been seen before! From this starting point, the poems could be as simple or as elaborate as the writer wanted, using imagination and descriptive language.

Given the young age of the entrants, we have tried to include as many poems as possible. Here at Young Writers we believe that seeing their work in print will inspire a love of reading and writing and give these young poets the confidence to develop their skills in the future. Poetry is a wonderful way to introduce young children to the idea of rhyme and rhythm and helps learning and development of communication, language and literacy skills.

These young poets have used their creative writing abilities, sentence structure skills, thoughtful vocabulary and most importantly, their imaginations, to make their poems and the animals within them come alive. I hope you enjoy reading them as much as we have.

Vicki Skelton

I Am A Parrot

On Thursday I was flying around
I could see an elephant stomping on
the ground
A crocodile with big teeth snaps
As a hunter sets some traps
The hippo plays in the mud
The rhino stomps with a thud
A parrot cleans its feathers
As the giraffe plays in all weathers.

Hollie Grace Kimber (6)
Barrow Hall Orchard CE Primary School, Loughborough

Fluff Ball

Big funky monkey, so big and chunky.
This monkey is very big and hairy.
He lives in the deep, dark jungle.
He has a mum and a dad,
He has a grandma.
He was called Fluffball.
He was a great boy,
I wish he was my best friend.
I wish I could swing as high as him.

Enzo Lee Preston (6)
Barrow Hall Orchard CE Primary School, Loughborough

Parrot

A parrot is pretty
A parrot has colourful feathers
A parrot can talk
A parrot can be in a zoo
A parrot is dangerous
A parrot is friendly
A parrot eats wild hamsters
A parrot has a hooked beak
A parrot is always busy
A parrot is always feeding its baby.

Isaac Carter (6)
Barrow Hall Orchard CE Primary School, Loughborough

The Parrot Spies

P ink flamingoes balancing in the pond
A long, dangly giraffe holding its head up in the sky
R oaring of a lion
R attling its skin, it's a snake
O n the prowl a tiger hunts
T he parrot spies all the fun in the jungle.

Esme Bradwell-Aumais (7)
Barrow Hall Orchard CE Primary School, Loughborough

The Bad Monkey

Monkeys are furry and brown
They swing high and you can't see them
Monkeys are slow and big
Monkeys are dark
Monkeys sing loud
Monkeys are very stinky
Monkeys have very big toes
Monkeys are chunky
Monkeys are bad
Monkeys are itchy.

Charlie Baker (5)
Barrow Hall Orchard CE Primary School, Loughborough

Flappy Parrots

P arrots fly in the sky
A parrot squawks with its sharp beak
R acing in the sky, parrots say goodbye
R olling in the leaves to get free
O n a branch it eats its berries
T igers roar, hippos snore at parrots.

Alex Broadhead (6)
Barrow Hall Orchard CE Primary School, Loughborough

Extremely Big Elephants

E xtremely heavy
L azy
E normous ears
P retty messy in the mud
H aving trouble touching his toes
A lligators want to eat elephants
N eeds to gnash its tusks
T ippy toes away.

Harry McQuade (6)
Barrow Hall Orchard CE Primary School, Loughborough

Parrot Snap

P ecking the trees making the jungle shake
A parrot gliding through the sky
R ound the jungle with its beautiful
feathers falling
R ainbow feathers fluffy and soft
O n a sunny day
T he parrot squawks.

Imogen Tormey (6)
Barrow Hall Orchard CE Primary School, Loughborough

The Chunky Monkey

The chunky monkey was swinging to his friend's house
But he saw a tiger
So he stopped
The tiger stopped
He ran away
But he passed the bananas
So he turned around
Ate some bananas
But then he finally got there.

George Oscar Camarco (7)
Barrow Hall Orchard CE Primary School, Loughborough

Pretty Parrots

The parrot soars through the dark,
dark jungle
The parrot shrieks through the trees
The parrot is flying, wait what can it see?
The parrot's feathers shine like a rainbow
The parrot is beautiful flying free.

Freya Close (7)
Barrow Hall Orchard CE Primary School, Loughborough

The Rich Monkey

The funky monkey was climbing in the trees
Peeling bananas just like me
I like climbing in the jungle
Cuddling my toy muggle
I am a rich monkey
I am the coolest guy in town
I am the best, I am a noun.

Sienna Boyles (6)
Barrow Hall Orchard CE Primary School, Loughborough

The Elephant

E normous tusks
L ong trunk
E ars are flappy
P ouring water
H e stomps around
A mazing trunk
N ight-time the elephant sleeps
T ogether in a heap.

Kole James Levett (6)
Barrow Hall Orchard CE Primary School, Loughborough

Parrots That Squawk

P arrots like to peck and fly
A parrot zooms in the sky
R iding on a cloud
R ocking in the trees, it's proud
O pening nuts with its beak
T ree-pecking parrot.

Zack Porter-Hamilton (6)
Barrow Hall Orchard CE Primary School, Loughborough

Fluff Ball

The funky monkey up on the wall
He had a great fall off the wall
He found a nut at the hut
He was swinging all the way home
He found his mum and dad
Roasting nuts and a nut that
was enormous.

Joe Hunt (6)
Barrow Hall Orchard CE Primary School, Loughborough

Jungle Explorer

The monkey is in the tree
It is funny and hairy
It always jumps in the trees
The trees are big and wide
It can always fit a monkey inside
The monkey is brown
Sometimes he cuddles up with me.

Gracie Bowman (6)
Barrow Hall Orchard CE Primary School, Loughborough

The Parrot

P retty parrot pecks plums
A parrot's feathers are soft
R ight up high in the trees
R ushes through crowds
O n a branch eats fruit
T rees are its home.

Max Hill (6)
Barrow Hall Orchard CE Primary School, Loughborough

Parrots Are Colourful

Amazing colours shine around the amazing,
colourful parrot
Above it flies through the trees
Its feathers move in the breeze
It stops to eat its nuts and fruit
Do you think the parrot's cute?

James Prevost (6)
Barrow Hall Orchard CE Primary School, Loughborough

The Snake

Once there was a snake, green and bright
It came out from the rocks
And gave us a fright
It gave us a hiss and sat up on the rocks
And slithered away
It got scared.

Megan Bailey (6)
Barrow Hall Orchard CE Primary School, Loughborough

Hissss

S lithering snake curling round trees
N aughty, hissing snake
A ngry, thirsty snake
K ind sun warms the snake
E xtremely enormous tongue.

Oscar James Hall (6)
Barrow Hall Orchard CE Primary School, Loughborough

The Hairy Monkey

The hairy monkey lives in a tree
This is where he goes for a wee
The hairy monkey swings all day
He likes to play
The hairy monkey eats bananas in
his pyjamas.

Wayne Finney (6)
Barrow Hall Orchard CE Primary School, Loughborough

From The Parrot's Eye

When I soar through the sky
I see the elephants stomping by
The monkeys swinging in the trees
Be careful of the bees
The tiger roars
The hippo snores.

Owen Burr (6)
Barrow Hall Orchard CE Primary School, Loughborough

Fluffy Monkey

Fluffy monkey is crazy all day
He throws bananas all day
He swings in the trees all day
He scratches his fluffy fur all day
He hides in the jungle all day.

Hermione Brayne (6)
Barrow Hall Orchard CE Primary School, Loughborough

I Love My Little Snake

My little snake is slippery
My little snake slithers
My little snake eats rats for breakfast
My little snake sleeps in the sun
I love my little snake.

Evie Newby (6)
Barrow Hall Orchard CE Primary School, Loughborough

Untitled

My little snake slithering around the trees
Looking at the green leaves
While I'm sticking my tongue out
Looking round the jungle trying to find rats.

Maisie Ann Flowers (7)
Barrow Hall Orchard CE Primary School, Loughborough

A Beautiful Rainbow Parrot

A beautiful rainbow parrot pecks some fruit
With his beak he makes a toot
He flies around to and fro
Watching monkeys swinging on slimy vines
as they go.

Samuel Johnson (7)
Barrow Hall Orchard CE Primary School, Loughborough

Squawker

The parrot zooms through the sky
His little wings go by
The parrot pecks the fruit
As it picks up a root
The parrot squawks and it talks and talks.

Kimberley Garner (6)
Barrow Hall Orchard CE Primary School, Loughborough

Monkeys

Monkeys are too fast if we are trying to
catch them
Monkeys are furry
Monkeys are the best at seeing
Swinging monkeys are very good at
swinging high.

Ben Whitehouse (5)
Barrow Hall Orchard CE Primary School, Loughborough

Funky

The monkey can climb higher than a bee
The more that he climbs the more he
can see
He is cheeky and funny, chunky and cute
I love monkeys.

Taylor Brooks (6)
Barrow Hall Orchard CE Primary School, Loughborough

Snake

S lithering snake
N ew skin tomorrow
A rat for dinner
K eeps its eggs hot
E ats small animals every day.

Leah Smith (6)
Barrow Hall Orchard CE Primary School, Loughborough

Snake

S lithering along in the
N ight
A slimy serpent slithers
K ing of the reptiles
E ating little animals.

Owen Spickett (7)
Barrow Hall Orchard CE Primary School, Loughborough

Monkey

The monkey is as funny as me
He likes climbing in the trees
Just like a bee
The monkey is as hairy as a bear
He looks very fair.

Amy Vaughan (5)
Barrow Hall Orchard CE Primary School, Loughborough

My Little Snake

My little snake slithers around my home and it slithers upstairs
Snake found a mouse, what a treat
My snake fell asleep happily.

Mia Cronin-Clarke (6)
Barrow Hall Orchard CE Primary School, Loughborough

The Monkey

The monkey was going to the beach
He took a milkshake with him
Also a McDonald's box
It was chicken nuggets and chips.

Ewan Harriman (6)
Barrow Hall Orchard CE Primary School, Loughborough

Fun Monkey

The monkey is funky
The monkey is big and fun
The monkey is cheeky
I love my monkey
My monkey is funny.

Felicity Bower (6)
Barrow Hall Orchard CE Primary School, Loughborough

The Funky Monkey

The funky monkey in a tree
Swinging high in the sky
He comes to play in the trees
It is a sunny day.

Tane Brown (6)
Barrow Hall Orchard CE Primary School, Loughborough

Snake

Slithery snake
Silly snake
Sequin scales
Slimy skin
Sticky tongue
Slithers up a tree.

Lottie Cavanagh (6)
Barrow Hall Orchard CE Primary School, Loughborough

Cheeky Monkey

The cheeky monkey swings all day
Singing all day long
The crazy monkey lives in the jungle.

Harry Kabi (6)
Barrow Hall Orchard CE Primary School, Loughborough

Slimy Snake

Slimy snake slithers slowly
Hiss sounds like a kettle
Spies on people.

Jasper King (6)
Barrow Hall Orchard CE Primary School, Loughborough

Monkeys

M onkeys eat delicious brown nuts
O n the trees, sneaky brown monkeys steal
yellow bananas like tall giraffes steal
leaves from trees
N o monkeys eat fresh, juicy, spiky
pineapples for tea
K ing monkey sits in his humongous red,
golden, shiny chair all day long
E very monkey eats delicious, fresh, shiny
yellow bananas
Y ucky, yellow bananas medium monkeys
do not eat
S ometimes monkeys eat fresh, brown
coconuts instead of delicious, fresh,
yellow, shiny, golden bananas.

Harry Hanvey (6)
Corby Old Village Primary School, Corby

Panda

P andas are huge, nearly like a boulder and
a very big zap
A panda can eat bamboo as fast as a blue
lightning bolt going to crash onto a huge
house
N o animal can eat huge bamboo as fast as
a huge panda like a leopard
D o pandas eat bamboo? Of course they
do. Why? Because they like bamboo
A ll a panda would eat is a huge bamboo
stick like my mum.

Morgan Fournier (6)
Corby Old Village Primary School, Corby

My Animal Poem

Butterflies smell as beautiful as
pink perfume
Butterflies fly high in the sky
Butterflies look as colourful as
mixed-up paint
Butterflies come out to play when it's hot
and sunny
Butterflies smell like enormous sunflowers
Butterflies like the taste of summer flowers
Busy, beautiful, bouncing butterflies.

Joanna Sandy (7)
Corby Old Village Primary School, Corby

My Animal Poem

D olphins can jump as high as a kangaroo
O n the sea is a dolphin
L eaping dolphins jump over the waves
P rancing and dancing is a dolphin looking at me
H ow can dolphins jump in the calm, pretty sea
I s a dolphin looking at me?
N ow to eat fish and jellyfish.

Eden Ruby Classick (6)
Corby Old Village Primary School, Corby

My Animal Poem

Butterflies are as smooth as silk
Butterflies can fly really, really fast
As fast as a cheetah
Butterflies can fly up to Heaven
Butterflies can fly as fast as cats can run.
Even faster
Butterflies can talk as quiet as a mouse
Butterflies can do tricks in the air.

Layla Mai Napier (7)
Corby Old Village Primary School, Corby

My Animal Poem

Cats smell like rotting fish
Cats are fluffy like my mum's slippers
Cats can run as fast as a leopard
Cats are a man's best friend
Cats can hear a mouse running around
my house
Cute, cuddly, creepy cats
Cats are the same as tigers.

Stasiu Czarnecki (7)
Corby Old Village Primary School, Corby

Polar Bears

Polar bears feel as fluffy as a cushion
Polar bears eat orange fish
Polar bears go out to hunt for wolves
Polar bears smell like fresh ice
Polar bears are fearless
Polar bears taste like white slippers
Polar bears are as white as a mountain.

Casey-Leigh Sellars (6)
Corby Old Village Primary School, Corby

Monkey

Monkeys smell like fifty bananas and
nine flies
Monkeys feel smooth and furry, huggable,
soft too
Monkeys look cute and look as brown as
some brown bread
Monkeys make a sound, oo-oo-aa-aa
Brown small monkey moves like a
man would.

Alex Lazarov (6)
Corby Old Village Primary School, Corby

Rabbit

R abbits can jump everywhere any time
A rabbit can hide in the burrow
B ump, bump, rabbits can jump
B ong, bong, look at the rabbit it can
scratch
I can see a fast, jumping rabbit
T asty grass you eat.

Ricardo Da Costa (6)
Corby Old Village Primary School, Corby

Rabbit

R abbits are as fluffy as a teddy
A rabbit eats carrots
B ut they are as white as a sheep
B ut it jumps really high like a frog
I t runs fast and loves to jump
T he rabbit is as cuddly as a blanket.

Alice Josephine Jane Logue (6)
Corby Old Village Primary School, Corby

My Animal Poem

Crocodiles eating fish and they're slimier than some mud
Crocodiles are as spiky as corners
They taste like water because they live in water
They smell like mud because they sleep in mud sometimes.
They taste like soft, soft mud.

Zak Graham (7)
Corby Old Village Primary School, Corby

Rabbit

R abbits are cuddly and fluffy
A nd they run as fast as a cheetah
B rown and black it could be
B ouncing around to their burrow
I t munches green grass
T eeny, tiny rabbits have a fluffy tail.

Jamie Arthur Jones (6)
Corby Old Village Primary School, Corby

My Animal Poem

R abbits are all cuddly like a teddy bear
A lways running through the grass
B ig, fluffy bears
B ack because they want food
I think they're teddies
T hey are always eating carrots.

Cassie Leanne Taylor (6)
Corby Old Village Primary School, Corby

My Animal Poem

R unning as quick as a flash
A re fabulous pets
B reakfast will be carrots
B lack, white or brown
I n the garden they live
T aking all the flowers
S tressing the dog.

Blake Lawman-Warren (6)
Corby Old Village Primary School, Corby

My Animal Poem

Cats eat fish for their dinner
Cats can do acrobatics
Some cats can climb trees
Some cats are playful or not
Cats are playful like puppies
Cats are as big as a little rock
Cats are as cute as a baby bear.

Amelia Mitchell (6)
Corby Old Village Primary School, Corby

My Animal Poem

D ogs lick you with their wet and cold
tongue
O h, the dog is growling
G rowling dogs can do tricks
S ometimes dogs like you.

Nikolas Stankovic (7)
Corby Old Village Primary School, Corby

Dinosaur

Dinosaurs smell like old trash cans
Dinosaurs dig, dig through the ground
Dinosaurs look like the enormous Titanic
Dinosaurs are as big as a house.

James Carlton (6)
Corby Old Village Primary School, Corby

Piglets

Piglets eat crunchy hay
Piglets are sparkly pink
Piglets run as fast as their mum
Piglets smell like stinky mud
Piglets sound very cute.

Jamie Mason (6)
Corby Old Village Primary School, Corby

Polar Bear

P owerful polar bear
O nly lives in the cold, wintry Arctic
L ooks for animals in a flash
A ir in the Arctic is very, very, very cold
R eady for hunting delicious prey

B ig, rough polar bear
E xtremely beautiful as a graceful swan
A lways looks after her cubs
R uns with her spread out paws.

Lola Jolley (6)
Hardingstone Academy, Northampton

All About Tigers!

S tripes as stripy as a stripy rug
T igers only live in the green grasslands
R unning tigers can run as fast as a horse
I t has sharp, fierce claws, as sharp as a
knife
P erfect orange fur
E legant as a swan
S cary roar is as loud as an elephant's
stompy feet.

Ellie Nichols (7)
Hardingstone Academy, Northampton

Jaguar Power

J aws with large teeth like a sword
A ctive body like a monkey
G entle, soft fur like a fluffy mattress
U gly, sharp teeth like a witch
A nnoying, fast body like a race happening
R acing jaguar like it's against a cheetah.

Erin Whitwam (6)
Hardingstone Academy, Northampton

Hippo Poem

I have a long body and four legs
I have a bumpy back and I'm tall
I have big teeth
I have small legs
I have big feet
I have a big head
What am I?

Charlie Rossetti (6)
Hardingstone Academy, Northampton

Snake It Up!

I slither on the ground
I am slimy
I have a large head and small eyes
I have a long body
I wrap myself around enemies
I am long but flat
What am I?

Hudson Wigley (6)
Hardingstone Academy, Northampton

Live In Fairy Land

I have a horn on top of my head
I live in a Fairy Land
I sound like this: naaaa
I am a magical creature
I like people who care for me
What am I?

Ellie-May State (6)
Hardingstone Academy, Northampton

Swinging Monkey

I feel soft
I look like a black thing
I sound like a really loud car
I live in the zoo or the jungle
I have two hands and two feet
What am I?

Josie Jacqueline Theresa Bell (6)
Hardingstone Academy, Northampton

Pat Bear

I am big and I am fluffy
I have four legs and ginormous back legs
I have sharp teeth
I have a brown body
I have tiny black eyes
What am I?

Mylee Jo Jenkins (6)
Hardingstone Academy, Northampton

Buzzing Bee

I have black spots
I buzz around
I take honey to my home
I can't talk
I have four legs
I have two antennae
What am I?

Angel-Marie Addae-Kyeremeh (6)
Hardingstone Academy, Northampton

Parrot

I am multicoloured like a rainbow
I eat hard nuts and juicy fruit
I live in the rainforest
I feel soft and feathery
What am I?

Ava Whitwam (6)
Hardingstone Academy, Northampton

Bouncy

I've got two bouncy legs
I have babies in my soft pouch
I look like a rabbit and a hare
I live in hot Australia
What am I?

Saran Singh Basra (6)
Hardingstone Academy, Northampton

In The Water

I am long, green and scaly
I have big, snappy, sharp teeth
I live in the wet and damp jungle
I am extremely sneaky
What am I?

Molly Whitwam (6)
Hardingstone Academy, Northampton

Laughing Hyena

I am covered in fur
I have four legs
I laugh all the time
I walk on four legs
I live in the African savannah
What am I?

Brooke Lee (7)
Hardingstone Academy, Northampton

Look Away

I look like a cat
I chase cats
I feel so soft
And I am covered in patterns
I guide people if they are blind
What am I?

Evelyn Jaina King (6)
Hardingstone Academy, Northampton

Untitled

I am stripy
I live in the dry grassland
I look like a horse
I eat juicy leaves
I live in a herd
What am I?

Lily Grace Masterson (6)
Hardingstone Academy, Northampton

At The Zoo

I saw a sloth moving his slow legs
I heard a mighty lion roaring
I felt a stripy zebra sleeping under the tree.

I saw a monkey swinging from vine to vine
I felt a slithering snake going past big trees
I heard an elephant stomping his feet.

I heard a black panther growling
I saw a bear climbing a tree
I felt the tough skin of the mighty elephant.

I saw a pony jumping over poles
I heard a blue whale splashing
I felt the tall, tall, tall neck of the giraffe.

Maryam O'Doherty (7)
Leicester Islamic Academy, Leicester

At The Zoo

I saw a brown horse neighing
I heard an orange tiger roaring
I felt a white pony eating leaves.

I saw a colourful parrot flying
I heard a big bear growling
I felt a spiky porcupine moving slowly.

I saw a green frog hopping
I heard a little penguin splashing
I felt a cute duck quacking.

I saw a massive wolf running
I heard a big lion roaring
I felt a red butterfly flying.

Hannah Dedat (7)
Leicester Islamic Academy, Leicester

At The Zoo

I saw a grey elephant staring at me
I heard a golden lion snoring
I felt a stripy zebra eating grass.

I saw a brown monkey swinging his arms
I heard a dark brown bear growling
I felt a light brown chimpanzee laughing.

I saw a grey hippo splashing water
I heard a yellow giraffe munching leaves
I felt a spiky hedgehog walking slowly.

Danh Alghamdi (6)
Leicester Islamic Academy, Leicester

At The Zoo

I saw the golden lion eating meat.
I heard a stripy tiger roaring.
I felt a black and white zebra neighing.

I saw a brown bear growling.
I heard an elephant trumpeting.
I felt a fluffy wolf howling.

I saw a colourful parrot squawking.
I heard a green crocodile snapping.
I felt a yellow duck quacking.

Harun Waseer (7)
Leicester Islamic Academy, Leicester

Untitled

Octopus, octopus swimming in the sea.
What do you see?
I can see a crab.
Octopus, octopus where do you live?
I live in the cave.
Octopus, octopus what do you eat?
Seaweed.

Oliver Mura (6)
Redwell Primary School, Wellingborough

Little Fish Who Plays With Me

Rainbowfish, rainbowfish play with me.
Little fish eat with me.
Little fish and me go to see Octopus.
Rainbowfish, rainbowfish play with me.
Little fish I like you.

Madison Norris (5)
Redwell Primary School, Wellingborough

Octopus

Octopus, octopus swimming in the sea.
Octopus, octopus you are so wise.
Octopus, octopus you are big.
Octopus, octopus having tea in a café.

Abigail Brewer (5)
Redwell Primary School, Wellingborough

Rainbow Fish

Rainbowfish, rainbowfish so shiny.
Rainbowfish, rainbowfish you're purple.
Rainbowfish, rainbowfish you're
so beautiful.

Jai Singh (5)
Redwell Primary School, Wellingborough

Untitled

Octopus, octopus are you wise?
Octopus, octopus are you inky?
Where do you live?
Are you squidgy?

Liam Wentzel (5)
Redwell Primary School, Wellingborough

Octopus

Octopus, octopus so clever.
Octopus, octopus please play with me.
Octopus, octopus eating seaweed.

Luca Ghiorghita (5)
Redwell Primary School, Wellingborough

Starfish

Starfish, starfish please play with me.
Starfish, starfish so clever.
Starfish, starfish so cute.

Christopher Orekoya (5)
Redwell Primary School, Wellingborough

Octopus

Octopus, octopus having some tea.
Octopus, octopus swimming in the sea.
Eating a pea in the sea.

Mason Brindle (5)
Redwell Primary School, Wellingborough

Mr Starfish

Starfish, starfish in the blue sea.
You are fat and orange.
Thick and lumpy too.

Dylan Edward Hughes (5)
Redwell Primary School, Wellingborough

My Mighty Creatures

S pecial creatures crouch along but mine is the best
A pples are being eaten by my animal quickly today
F og is getting in the way of animals but mine has fog lights.
A nts are crawling and biting big animals but mine can kill all the ants so mine can't be bitten.
R oaring, crawling everywhere my animal's so mighty
I gloos can be built by him, oh how strong and mighty.

Sofija Trusele (7)
Richmond Primary School, Hinckley

Untitled

My big animal likes to wiggle his tail.
It likes to lick his legs.
It wants to be lazy, crazy and silly.
My animal likes to run and walk.
It likes Mum the best.
My animal likes to play with toys and play with babies.
My animal likes to walk in the dark and light woods.
My animal likes to read a book.
My animal likes to play with a ball.

Tayla-Brooke Coley (6)
Richmond Primary School, Hinckley

The Snow Rabbit

He looks soft and fluffy.
He feels hairy.
He has white ears.
He sounds growly and super loud.
His voice is loud and clear.
He sleeps all night long.
He loves to play all day.
My pet is cute and cuddly.
My pet likes to dance a lot.
Pets are cuddly and cute.
My pet does live in a cave.

Lola Cuthbert (5)
Richmond Primary School, Hinckley

Safari Poem

Animals are at the zoo
Fastest cheetah in the world
Most annoying cheetah in the world
Roaring in the safari
I like the safari park
I will always like the safari park
It is the best safari park ever
In the whole world.
Thank you for this beautiful safari park
And the lovely animals.

Viola Proctor (6)
Richmond Primary School, Hinckley

Safari

S potty turtle lion crept along
A dog's tail swooshing
F our-eyed turtle lion zebra looks out
A big turtle lion zebra runs, jumps and falls over
R oar the turtle lion zebra
I t runs along then lies down and sleeps.

Khloe Mason (6)
Richmond Primary School, Hinckley

Safari

S arah loves to eat Marmite.
A favourite food will do.
F our zebra legs, a twisted tail, a scaly head the best match.
A n elephant is his best friend
R ipe fruit, mmm, for Sarah.
I like animals do you?

Carly Powers (6)
Richmond Primary School, Hinckley

Safari

S cary animals are bad because they scratch.
A mazing animals are good animals.
F ast animals can be good.
A ngry animals are bad.
R unning in zoos is against the zoo rules.
I n the zoo animals are lazy.

Janie Siobhan Finch (5)
Richmond Primary School, Hinckley

The Squirrel

A squirrel is fast,
He runs up a tree,
He looks down at you and me,
He buries his nuts in the ground,
In the winter to be found,
His tail is fluffy and red,
He has pointy ears on his head,
He likes to sleep in his leafy bed.

Patti Hajda (6)
Richmond Primary School, Hinckley

Safari

S traight body and long neck
A kangaroo tail wiggling around
F our long legs walking around me
A lion saying grrrr
R abbits jumping around everywhere
I have made my name up, it's Chloe.

Georgia-Mai Bennett (7)
Richmond Primary School, Hinckley

Safari

S afari park is the best.
A nimals run up and down.
F at animals sleep all day long
A nnoying animals snore all day long
R unning in the zoo is fun
I n the zoo animals make a lot of noise.

Mia Louise Roberts (5)
Richmond Primary School, Hinckley

Safari

S peedy leopards in the zoo jumping up
A mazing elephants are marching
F ancy tigers having a picnic
A nnoying lions telling jokes
R oaring bears eating meat
I love this zoo and so do you.

Demi-Leigh Wright (5)
Richmond Primary School, Hinckley

Untitled

He has a short tail.
He has a waggy tail.
He looks colourful.
He has scary eyes.
He has a fluffy tail.
He has a trunk
He looks nice.
He looks lovely.
He looks so lovely.
He looks really lovely.

Emily Jean-Gray Ahearne (5)
Richmond Primary School, Hinckley

The Animal Poem

S potty body hops along.
A long grey tail wagging behind.
F luffy ears are very fluffy.
A fishy breath is very stinky.
R oar goes the cheetah.
I nto bed goes the cheetah.

Scarlett Goodall-Heath (6)
Richmond Primary School, Hinckley

Untitled

He has a sharp beak
He eats fish for his tea
He lives in the sea
He is nice
He lives with his mummy
He loves splashing in the sea
He loves swimming with his mummy
He swims better than his mummy.

Phoebe Eliza Guest (5)
Richmond Primary School, Hinckley

Safari

S peedy Elly the whale is very silly
A frican animals have four legs
F ast friends I really like you
A frican animals are amazing
R ats are small
I n this safari park.

Ralph McManus (6)
Richmond Primary School, Hinckley

The Animal Poem

S tomp, stomp she goes and she can't stop.
A big, big rat comes by
F ear or fright
A nd a tiger with big teeth
R unning by like a flash
I fell and said that hurt.

Erin Barnes (6)
Richmond Primary School, Hinckley

Safari

S afari park
A frican animals are amazing
F astest cheetah in the universe
A nimals are nice to look at
R ats are small
I n the safari park you see animals.

Lewis Tompkins (6)
Richmond Primary School, Hinckley

Super Safari Park

S uper slow
A mazing animals on the loose
F antastic flexibility
A ngry feeling
R oaring always
I like my safari park and I always will.

Rebecca McEwan (6)
Richmond Primary School, Hinckley

Safari

S cruffy mane is good
A fraid of thunder
F red is his name
A fraid of lightning
R ude when he's mad
I 'd leave him alone.

Jack Dunphy (6)
Richmond Primary School, Hinckley

The Biggest Safari Park

S afari park
A mazing giraffes
F antastic hyenas
A nnoying lions
R hinos are the biggest
I n the cave giraffes eat apples.

Maisie Giles (6)
Richmond Primary School, Hinckley

Safari

S afari animals big and small
A fraid of you
F ight you, purr at you
A ngry and love you
R un fast
I n the little cave.

Chloe Louise King (6)
Richmond Primary School, Hinckley

Safari

S potty dots running through the grass
A swinging tail
F or dinner he has bones
A best friend
R ed tail
I n my car.

Tyler Haigh-Cufflin (6)
Richmond Primary School, Hinckley

The Animal Poem

S tripy blue body.
A tiger head.
F our legs.
A dog's tail, big and fluffy.
R oars loud.
I t has sharp claws.

Armani Kabodi (6)
Richmond Primary School, Hinckley

Safari

S earching for food
A mazing strips
F eels greedy
A mazing feeling
R eady for the hunt
I 'm not scared.

Mollie Elizabeth Mattock (6)
Richmond Primary School, Hinckley

The Squirrel

A squirrel is fast
He runs up the tree
He looks down at you and me
His tail is fluffy and red
He likes to sleep in his leafy bed.

Brooklyn Wyatt (5) & Angel
Richmond Primary School, Hinckley

The Squirrel

He runs up a tree
He looks down at you and me
His tail is fluffy and red
He has pointy ears
He likes to sleep in his leafy bed.

Ella Osborne (5)
Richmond Primary School, Hinckley

Safari

S illy pig
A mazing pig
F at pig
A nnoying pig
R ound pig
I n the swimming pool.

Kara Carter (6)
Richmond Primary School, Hinckley

The Squirrel

A squirrel runs up a tree.
He looks down at you and me.
His tail is fluffy and red.
He likes to sleep in his leafy bed.

Joshua Tubby (5)
Richmond Primary School, Hinckley

Untitled

S peedy dog
A ngry dog
F at dog
A nnoying dog
R ound tummy
I n its bed.

Warren Moore
Richmond Primary School, Hinckley

Untitled

He has a long trunk
He has a short tail
He has big feet
He has hard skin
He has big ears
He is very heavy.

Lacey Granger (7)
Richmond Primary School, Hinckley

The Fastest Cat

He is short and friendly
Soft and furry
He hunts all night sometimes
He can run really fast
He is yellow.

Rocky Wailoo (5)
Richmond Primary School, Hinckley

Safari

S peedy
A mazing
F at
A ngry
R oaring
I ndestructible.

Leo Edward Wesley Hall (6)
Richmond Primary School, Hinckley

Untitled

My kangaroo has some fur
He is cute
He jumps around
All day long
He likes carrots to eat.

Lily Watson (7)
Richmond Primary School, Hinckley

Untitled

My animal is fluffy.
It feels soft.
As loud as a kettle.
It swings around.

Toby Rowan
Richmond Primary School, Hinckley

Butterfly

My butterfly looks furry
My butterfly feels soft
My butterfly sounds fluttery.

Keira Roche (5)
Richmond Primary School, Hinckley

Lion

He is fierce and strong
He has a fluffy orange mane
He can run very fast.

Archie Shorrock (5)
Richmond Primary School, Hinckley

Polar Bear

My polar bear looks blue
My polar blue feels cute
My polar bear sounds funny.

Oliver George Petherick (5)
Richmond Primary School, Hinckley

Snake

My snake looks slithery
My snake feels slippy
My snake sounds slimy.

Frazer Moore (5)
Richmond Primary School, Hinckley

The Giraffe

He has a very tall neck.
He has sharp claws.
He has huge legs.

Evan Joseph I'Anson (5)
Richmond Primary School, Hinckley

Untitled

My snake looks slimy
My snake feels soft
My snake sounds fierce.

Mitchell McCarthy (5)
Richmond Primary School, Hinckley

Snake

My snake looks green
My snake feels soft
My snake sounds scary.

Reuben Pankhurst (5)
Richmond Primary School, Hinckley

Zebra

My zebra looks stripy
My zebra feels soft
My zebra sounds fast.

Oliver Kinsey (5)
Richmond Primary School, Hinckley

Rainbow Animals

He's as soft as a picky polar bear
He's as colourful as a rainbow
He flies like an excited eagle
He eats like a crazy crocodile
He sounds like a fierce, dreadful dragon
He's as strong as steel
It's Fire, my cloud dragon.

James Wrigley (6)
Woodford CE Primary School, Kettering

Rainbow Spider Dog

It is as fluffy as a cloud
It is like a rainbow
It likes bones and it makes spiderwebs
It is like a lion, sneaking in your bedroom
It is my rainbow spider dog
It is called Hatboy.

Kai Edward Kitchener (7)
Woodford CE Primary School, Kettering

The Diplodocus Dragon

It is as dangerous as lava
It is as hot as fire
It eats meat like a crocodile
It breathes like a goose
It likes to go to a castle like a knight
It's a diplodocus dragon.

Jake Bester (6)
Woodford CE Primary School, Kettering

Red Puppy Paws

She has blue glasses
She is as cute as a baby
She is as light as wind
She is as small as an ant
She is as fresh as a flower
She is a mix-up
My puppy called Cosmo.

Freya Bradbrook (6)
Woodford CE Primary School, Kettering

The Cute Sealion

Sealion smells like fish.
It goes in the ocean
And it swims in the water
As fast as a fish.
As smooth as the deep blue sea,
As cute as a cat,
The sealion is so pretty.

Anya-Lea Swain (6)
Woodford CE Primary School, Kettering

Fluffy Animals

As hot as fire
He's as colourful as a rainbow
As fluffy as a cloud
His eyes are as big as a coconut
He's as strong as steel
It's my diplodocus owl.

Holly Fasham (6)
Woodford CE Primary School, Kettering

The Patchy Dog

He is as soft as silk
He is as funny as a flamingo
He is as bouncy as a ball
He is as useful as a servant
He is as patchy as a panda
Yes, it is a dog.

Miri-Mae Sturdy (6)
Woodford CE Primary School, Kettering

About A Pig

It's as pink as a pink pen
His ears are as pointy as a needle
It's as cuddly as a bear
His legs are as long as a giraffe's neck
It's a pig.

Bella Ward (6)
Woodford CE Primary School, Kettering

About The Cheeky Cheetah

It's as fast as a car
It's as spotty as Mrs Steventon's trousers
It's as big as a door
It's as orange as a peach
It's a cheetah.

Eryn Billingham (5)
Woodford CE Primary School, Kettering

My Creature

He is as fast as a racing car
He is as stinky as a sweaty sock
He is as strong as a lion
He is as tall as a house
His eyes are as small as marbles.

Alexie Ruby May Clutterbuck (6)
Woodford CE Primary School, Kettering

A Colourful Horse

It's as pink as a berry
It's as blue as a sticker
It's as cute as a bunny
It's as black as a chair
It is a horse.

Aiden Linger (5)
Woodford CE Primary School, Kettering

Untitled

Lion is colourful
It's as colourful as a bird
It's as evil as a dinosaur
It flies like a seagull
It runs like a bear.

Ollie Harry Carter (6)
Woodford CE Primary School, Kettering

Giraffe

Giraffes are tall
It has a long neck
Rainbow colours on my giraffe
Fierce
Friendly
Enormous.

Lily Stevens (6)
Woodford CE Primary School, Kettering

Untitled

It has a smooth body
It has soft legs
It has fluffy wool
It has a black head
It's a sheep.

Nathan John Davis (5)
Woodford CE Primary School, Kettering

My Sealion

It is scary, hairy and wet.
It has sharp teeth
And a slimy mouth.
It is faster than a dinosaur.

Tyler Hudnott (5)
Woodford CE Primary School, Kettering

A Sealion

It is as fast as a fish
It can do shows
It can do moves
It can swim
It's a sealion.

Kornel Wojtyla (5)
Woodford CE Primary School, Kettering

Young Writers Information

We hope you have enjoyed reading this book – and that you will continue to in the coming years.

If you're a young writer who enjoys reading and creative writing, or the parent of an enthusiastic poet or story writer, do visit our website www.youngwriters.co.uk. Here you will find free competitions, workshops and games, as well as recommended reads, a poetry glossary and our blog.

If you would like to order further copies of this book, or any of our other titles give us a call or visit **www.youngwriters.co.uk.**

Young Writers, Remus House, Coltsfoot Drive, Peterborough, PER2 9BF
(01733) 890066

info@youngwriters.co.uk